P

Birds Bringing Words

by Danielle Melanee

Harcourt
SCHOOL PUBLISHERS

Cover, ©AP Photo/Las Vegas Sun, Aaron Mayes; p.3, ©Michael Newman/PhotoEdit; p.4, ©AP Photo/ Andrew Laker; p.5, ©Matthew Johnston/Alamy; p.6–7, ©Eastcott-Momatiuk/AnimalsAnimals; p.8, ©The Art Archive/Museo Prenestino Palestrina/Dagli Orti; p.9, ©Thomas Hoepker/Magnum Photos; p.10, ©AP Photo/Baever County Times, Peter Sabella; p.11, ©The Art Archive/Imperial War Museum; p.12, ©Boyer/Roger-Viollet The Image World; p.13, ©U.S. Army; p 14 ©Corbis.

Copyright © by Harcourt, Inc.

All rights reserved. No part of this publication may be reproduced or transmitted in any form or by any means, electronic or mechanical, including photocopy, recording, or any information storage and retrieval system, without permission in writing from the publisher.

Requests for permission to make copies of any part of the work should be addressed to School Permissions and Copyrights, Harcourt, Inc., 6277 Sea Harbor Drive, Orlando, Florida 32887-6777. Fax: 407-345-2418.

HARCOURT and the Harcourt Logo are trademarks of Harcourt, Inc., registered in the United States of America and/or other jurisdictions.

Printed in China

ISBN 10: 0-15-350456-0
ISBN 13: 978-0-15-350456-3

Ordering Options
ISBN 10: 0-15-350333-5 (Grade 3 Below-Level Collection)
ISBN 13: 978-0-15-350333-7 (Grade 3 Below-Level Collection)
ISBN 10: 0-15-357468-2 (package of 5)
ISBN 13: 978-0-15-357468-9 (package of 5)

If you have received these materials as examination copies free of charge, Harcourt School Publishers retains title to the materials and they may not be resold. Resale of examination copies is strictly prohibited and is illegal.

Possession of this publication in print format does not entitle users to convert this publication, or any portion of it, into electronic format.

11 12 13 14 15 0940 12 11 10

Pests or Heroes?

Have you seen pigeons before? Look on fences. Look at rooftops. Toss bread crumbs on the ground. Pigeons will come and eat.

Some people think pigeons are pests. Others disagree. They think pigeons are heroes.

Pigeons are part of history. They have saved lives. Let's find out more.

Finding Home

Pigeons are fast. They can fly fifty miles (80 km) an hour. They can turn and dive quickly.

There are some pigeons that have another skill. They are called "homing" pigeons.

What does *homing* mean? Put the birds anywhere. They will find their way home.

How do they do it? No one is sure.
They may use the sun. They may
follow the stars.

What if it is cloudy? Pigeons may
use the earth.

When people need to know
which direction they are going,
they use a compass. Pigeons do
not have compasses. They may
feel the earth's pull, though.

The sun, earth, and stars may
help, too. They tell directions, but
that isn't the whole answer.

What if you didn't know which
direction to go to get home? You
would need a map to figure it out.

Pigeons don't need maps. We
don't know why. They may use
scent. They may use sounds.
"Homing" is a mystery.

Lofts and Learning

Pigeons were used as messengers in 3000 B.C. People trained them to obey in ancient Egypt!

Genghis Khan ruled in the 1100s. His kingdom was very big. Pigeons carried his messages to faraway places.

Some people build houses for pigeons. These houses are called lofts. Lofts can be any size. They should have food and water for the pigeons. That is important. The birds return to places where they know they have food.

Take a pigeon away from its loft. Then let it go. The bird flaps its wings. It is off! It never wanders.

It flies right back to the loft. Now it is home. It eats. It drinks. It feels safe.

Pigeons do not need someone to demonstrate this for them. They just know what to do.

Heroes

World War I began in 1914. There was no e-mail. There were no cell phones. The radio was new. It didn't always work. It couldn't send maps.

Armies needed to send messages quickly. Pigeons were the answer. Pigeon lofts were put on army bases and also right on the battlefields.

Soldiers wrote messages and drew maps during battles and while on patrol. They tied them to the legs of pigeons. Then they let them go. The pigeons took the messages to the lofts on the fields. Then they returned to the lofts on the army bases. People got the messages. They sent help.

Some birds even wore tiny cameras. They took photos from the air. The photos showed important information.

Some pigeons became famous. Cher Ami carried a message from soldiers in trouble during World War I. He was shot while flying, but he made it to his loft safely. The message saved many soldiers. Cher Ami was given a medal!

Maybe you know some people who lived during this war. They may have heard of these bird heroes that never whined. They always did a great job.

There is a statue in France. It is for pigeon war heroes. It thanks them. Homing pigeons saved many lives.

Think Critically

1. What do homing animals do?

2. "Some people think pigeons are pests." Is this statement a fact or an opinion? Why?

3. What problem did pigeons solve during World War I?

4. How do people think homing pigeons can do what they do?

5. Do you think that there's a need for pigeon messengers today? Explain your answer.

 Social Studies

Check It Out Pigeons were helpful during World War I. Find out which countries were in this war and make a list of them. Then find them on a map.

School-Home Connection Tell family members about homing pigeons. Then talk to family members about what you should do if you ever get lost.